# OPTIONAL ALTERNATIVE
# PUBLIC SCHOOLS

By Vernon H. Smith
Daniel J. Burke
Robert D. Barr

All of Indiana University

Library of Congress Catalog Card Number: 74-83880
Copyright © 1974 by The Phi Delta Kappa Educational Foundation
Bloomington, Indiana

# TABLE OF CONTENTS

## INTRODUCTION

One of the hallmarks of a democratic society is the choices its citizens have in important aspects of their daily lives. Citizens in a democracy should expect to have options in government and politics, products and markets, vocations and avocations, places of residence and of work, entertainment and recreation, medical and dental care, transportation, the mass media, education, religion, and social and family life. In all but one of these areas options are available in our contemporary society. For nearly 90% of the families in this country, there are no choices in elementary and secondary education.

Without choice, and even without parental consent, children and youth are assigned to specific schools and to specific classes within those schools. The same situation exists for some teachers and administrators who are assigned to specific schools within a district. This situation is both undemocratic and un-American.

Different people learn in different ways. Many children learn well in our traditional academic public schools. Some children learn better in the differently structured environment of the open school. Others learn better in a school developed on principles of behavior modification. And still others learn better in an individualized, continuous-progress school. The psychology of education—the study of how people learn—is relatively young, less than a century old. Complete theories of learning and corresponding theories of instruction are yet to be developed. What we do know today is that some children learn well in one setting while others learn well in a different setting.

If the lack of choice in public education is undemocratic, and if we know that some children would learn better in different types of schools, why do we assign all children in a neighborhood to one conventional school? The answer, we believe, is that the lack of options in public education is a historical accident. This country will soon be 200 years old. During the first 150 years and probably longer, more learning options were available than are available today.

Private schools have always existed for families who could afford them and parochial schools have existed for those who preferred them. But enrollment in nonpublic schools is at an all-time low today, indicating that these options are available to fewer and fewer students. In the agrarian and frontier society of our first 100 years, children could quit school, and did, for on-the-job training in farming and other occupations. Apprenticeships for children and youth were common.

During the next fifty years, as our society evolved from agrarian to industrial, opportunities for on-the-job training expanded, with many children employed in plants and factories. As late as 1900, twice as many school-age children were working as going to school, many of them under 10 years of age. Whether desirable or not, work was a legitimate learning alternative to schooling for our first 150 years. During this period evening schools were established in some communities to accommodate youths of age nine and over who were employed full time. As more adult laborers immigrated to this country, as labor unions developed, and as child labor laws were extended and enforced, apprenticeships, on-the-job training, and regular work for those of school age became scarcer and scarcer.

At the beginning of this century fewer than 10% of all youth in this country completed high school. Programs of high schools and the grammar schools were academically oriented to prepare those few who would finish high school to go on to college. It was widely recognized that many students did not learn well in this academic setting. Only a minority were expected to succeed. The development of vocational schools, therefore, was an effort to provide an option for many students who otherwise would have dropped out to face a declining (for school-age youth) job market. Optional evening schools survived in a few communities, but as the compulsory school age was extended, students were forced more and more to attend the public school to which they were assigned. By 1950, the vast majority of children and youth had no other option.

Within a relatively short time, certainly less than thirty years (1920-1950), those conventional schools which had been eliminating a majority of students before graduation from high school were expected to provide mass elementary and secondary education for all children and youth. As a nation we had committed our schools to an impossible task, but it took a while for educators, parents, and the general public to realize this.

## The Development of Optional Alternative Public Schools

Some communities recognized before others that the single standard school could not meet the needs of all students. Some communities saw the need for starting new schools for talented students, such as Bronx High School of Science in New York City (1938). Some communities provided for dropouts and potential dropouts schools such as the Metropolitan Youth Education Center in Denver (1964). Some communities wanted to change all schools, as in the move toward open elementary education in North Dakota (1965). Other communities attempted to provide optional schools, such as The Parkway plan in Philadelphia (1969).

By 1970, the need for alternatives to the conventional school was widely recognized. Many communities were developing alternative public schools to complement conventional schools in order to make the school systems within those communities more responsive to the needs of all children and youth. In many communities today students, parents, teachers, and administrators have choices among various optional alternative public schools. In the last few years several national reports on education have recommended the offering of alternative public schools. The 1973 *Report of the National Commission on the Reform of Secondary Education* urges that:

> Each district should provide a broad range of alternative schools and programs so that every student will have a meaningful educational option available to him.

The authors of this book have been working with the development of optional alternative public schools for a number of years.

We hope to show how these optional schools provide a means for making public education more responsive to the needs of children and youth in this decade and this century. We believe optional schools will become a vital part of the continuing search for compromise among the educational needs of the individual, of a democratic society, of a technological world, and of future generations.

## A DESCRIPTION OF OPTIONAL ALTERNATIVE PUBLIC SCHOOLS

When a community provides optional alternative public schools, the conventional school becomes one option. Usually it is the most popular option. An important advantage of offering optional schools is that this removes the requirement of consensus. Families satisfied with the conventional school still have that option, and for families who choose a different option, the risk is low. If the alternative proves to be unsatisfactory for some students, they can return to the conventional school. Alternative schools will not replace the conventional school; they will complement it so that the alternatives and the conventional school together will provide educational programs that are responsive to the needs of students.

### Types of Optional Alternative Public Schools

The optional schools have usually developed as responses to particular needs within their communities. No single model could encompass their diversity, but there are some common types into which the majority of optional alternative public schools would fit.

*Open schools* provide individualized learning experiences organized around interest or resource centers throughout the building. Open education is not new, but interest in open schools has been growing because of their popularity in Great Britain and because of recent developments in the psychology of learning. The St. Paul Open School is one example; housed in a refurbished warehouse, it enrolls 500 students in kindergarten through grade 12.

*Schools-without-walls* provide learning experiences throughout the community and offer increased interaction between school and community. Philadelphia's Parkway program, which opened in 1969, was the first and is probably the best known. Others include Metro in Chicago, Genesis (formerly Community High School) in Berkeley, and City School in Madison, Wisconsin.

*Learning centers* have a concentration of resources in one location available to all of the students in the community. These include magnet schools, educational parks, career education centers, and vocational and technical high schools. St. Paul has developed a network of learning centers at both elementary and secondary levels. Students spend part of the day in their home school and part in an optional learning center. The Skyline Center in Dallas provides learning experiences that cannot be offered in every high school—an aircraft hangar and airstrip, a computer center, and classes in Greek and Swahili.

*Continuation schools* make provision for students whose education has been (or might be) interrupted—drop-out centers, re-entry programs, pregnancy-maternity centers, evening and adult high schools, and street academies. The Metropolitan Youth Education Center, with four locations in Denver and Jefferson County, Colorado, and Pacific Shores High School in Manhattan Beach, California, both in operation for about ten years, have served the needs of thousands of students within their communities.

*Multicultural schools* emphasize cultural pluralism and ethnic and racial awareness; they usually serve a multicultural student body. Bilingual schools with optional enrollment are included in this category. SAND Everywhere in Hartford, Connecticut, is a multicultural elementary school in a former warehouse. Agora in Berkeley is a high school serving black, Chicano, and white students.

*Free schools* emphasize freedom for students and teachers to plan and implement their own learning experiences without conventional constraints. This term is frequently used to designate nonpublic alternative schools, but a few free schools are available by choice within public school systems in Berkeley, Minneapolis, and Philadelphia.

*Schools-within-a-school* operate when a small number of students and teachers are involved by choice in a different learning program. This category includes both the *minischool* within the building and the *satellite school* on another location but with administrative ties to the conventional school. Schools-within-schools usually belong to one of the six types above.

The *complex of alternative schools* has several optional alternative schools housed together in one building and usually under one administration. Haaren High School in New York City; Quincy II in Quincy, Illinois; New School in Cleveland Heights, Ohio; and Ravenswood High School in East Palo Alto, California, are all large high schools which consist of a number of alternative schools or minischools. The conventional program may or may not exist as one of the alternatives.

*Cooperative alternative schools* exist when one or more optional alternative schools are cooperatively funded and operated by several nearby school systems. In Hartford, Connecticut; Kent County, Michigan; and the Greater Philadelphia area, school districts have collaborated to offer optional schools to students from several communities.

Naturally there may be considerable overlapping among these categories. And some optional alternative public schools would not fit into any of these categories. The Alternative Education Center in Grand Rapids is a school based on behavior modification. The Pratt/Motley Schools in Minneapolis are continuous progress elementary schools. Some alternative public schools operate as voluntary integration models within their communities—in Louisville, St. Paul, Philadelphia, and Chicago, to name a few.

Special function schools that serve students who are assigned or referred without choice should not be considered alternative schools. A school to which disruptive students are assigned may be highly desirable in some communities, but it should not be confused with optional public schools.

### Common Characteristics

While alternative public schools have been developed in response to needs within their community, most share some of the following characteristics:

1. As previously stated, the school provides an option for students, parents, and teachers. Usually the choice is open to all within the community, but there must always be choice for some so that the alternative school has a voluntary clientele. The school population should reflect the socioeconomic and racial makeup of the entire community. There is no need for public alternative schools that are elite or racist.

2. The alternative school has as its reason for existence a commitment to be more responsive to some educational need within its community than the conventional schools have been.

3. The alternative school usually has more comprehensive goals and objectives than its conventional counterpart. While most alternative schools are concerned with developing basic skills and preparing students for college and vocations, they are also concerned with improving a student's self-concept, developing individual talent and uniqueness, understanding and encouraging cultural plurality and diversity, and preparing students for various roles in society—consumer, voter, critic, parent, spouse, and so on.

4. The alternative school is more flexible than conventional schools. It is therefore more responsive to planned evolution and change. Since alternatives are being developed in our age of accountability, they rely on feedback and formative evaluation in developing and modifying their curricula.

5. Alternative schools tend to be smaller than comprehensive high schools. The median enrollment in alternative public schools is under 200. Because they are smaller, alternatives tend to have fewer rules and bureaucratic constraints on students and teachers.

Considered collectively, these characteristics indicate that optional alternative schools do differ in significant ways from their conventional counterparts, but these differences are not nearly as significant as the total impact of optional schools on the school system. Each optional school, by being responsive to certain learning needs, helps to create a local school system that is more responsive to the needs of its community. The ultimate goal within any community should be to provide every parent with meaningful choices about his child's education.

## Psychological Considerations

Since children learn in different ways and at different times, alternative schools provide a natural arena for exploring the relationships among the learning styles of students, the instructional styles of teachers, and varying learning environments. Research on matching students' learning styles with certain environmental characteristics of conventional and alternative schools is already underway. In the near future it may be possible to design learning environments to meet specific learning needs and styles.

Meanwhile, teachers and others working in optional public schools frequently report beneficial side effects. One of these involves the psychology of choice. Students and parents are more loyal to a school they have chosen than one chosen for them. Teachers are too. Both teachers and administrators report a preference for the student body that is voluntary rather than compulsory. If multiple options are available within the community, the conventional school becomes one of the options, and it too benefits from a voluntary student enrollment and a voluntary teaching staff.

There is also a therapy of involvement associated with the optional schools. When parents, students, teachers, and administrators are involved in planning the program, they establish a healthy interaction which creates a spirit of cooperation hard to duplicate in other ways. This goes well beyond the conventional PTA meeting. If parents, students, or teachers are unhappy with the school system, discussing the need for alternatives provides an outlet for their feelings and a constructive way to use their energies to improve the system.

Whenever we talk with students or teachers from optional schools, they assure us that their school is more "humane" than the conventional school that they were in previously. At least part of this feeling is a response to the smaller size of the optional school. At the secondary level many of these students and teachers have come from high schools or junior high schools that enrolled over 1,000 students. Inhumaneness may be directly related to size. Certainly a school for 6,000 must have more rules and bureaucratic constraints than a school for sixty. In many optional schools students and teachers know the names of every student and every staff member.

Whether it is humaneness or choice, directors of optional alternative schools frequently report less truancy, less vandalism, fewer discipline problems, and less absenteeism. We have observed that both students and teachers tend to stay around after school hours and to show up on days when school is not in session. This all suggests that there are some desirable psychological differences associated with some optional public schools.

## Sociological Considerations

Earlier we indicated that choice in public education is consistent with democratic principles, but philosophy is only one part of the complex relationship between a democratic society and its educational system. During the last decade attempts have been made to decentralize the decision-making process in public education. In some communities students, teachers, principals, parents, and other lay citizens feel they have little or no voice in determining what goes on in their local schools. Developing optional public schools provides opportunities for decision making and community participation at the local level. In some communities today new partnerships are being formed among citizens and educators as they plan, develop, and operate optional alternative public schools. Community boards involving parents and other community members are an integral part of alternative public schools in Berkeley, Louisville, and St. Paul.

Optional public schools provide another level of control. When schools are available by choice, the community has control through the consumer—the individual family. Families either choose to send their children to a specific alternative school, or they do not. When only a few families select an optional school, obviously that community does not perceive the need for offering that alternative at that time. On the other hand, if thousands of families want their children in a particular school, this would indicate that the community needs more schools of that type. This is exactly what happened in Philadelphia when thousands of students applied for the few hundred openings at Parkway. Parkway quadrupled its original size by adding three new locations.

Unfortunately, there are still many more applicants for Parkway each year than the available openings.

Optional alternative public schools play a role in the search for solutions to some of our major social problems. In some communities, the optional school is a voluntary racial integration model. In other communities the optional school integrates different socioeconomic classes that would normally be segregated in neighborhood schools. Chicago's Metro, Louisville's Brown School, and the Cambridge Pilot School have voluntarily integrated student enrollments that represent each city's total population. The St. Paul Learning Centers provide racially integrated education in a city whose neighborhoods are racially segregated. Over 95% of the eligible families participate in this voluntary integration program. It is important to note here that the choices these St. Paul families make are educational choices. They choose the Automotive Transportation Learning Center because this educational experience is not available in their neighborhood school. This solution to segregation is quite different from the practice of busing students who do not want to go to schools that do not want to take them.

Many of the attempts to reform education in the last two decades were socially unacceptable because they sought to provide a reformed school for everyone. They required consensus. Even though many parents would like to see changes in the schools, they certainly would not all agree on exactly what those changes should be. The optional school provides a strategy for exploring different modes of education without requiring consensus or compulsion within the community.

## Economic Considerations

It is impossible to discuss public education without considering today's economic situation. During the past decade the cost of public education increased at a rate significantly faster than the increase in the national economy. It is unlikely that we will see such a massive increase in funds for public education again in this century.

Optional public schools usually operate on the same per pupil budgets as other schools at the same level within the same community. Some cost more, and many cost less, but in many communities conventional schools also vary in per pupil cost. Sometimes modest funds are necessary for planning and development; sometimes they are not. As a district moves to optional schools, there will probably be transitional expenses, just as there are added expenses each time a new conventional school is opened within the district. In many districts school boards and administrators have found ways to provide alternatives without significant added expense. Who really knows how much schooling should cost? The smaller alternative schools provide opportunities to vary organizational structure and staffing, which would be difficult to try in the larger conventional schools. The alternative school provides a way that a community can seek the optimum level of funding for its schools.

When a community makes multiple options available there is an open market in education, and the consumer—the student and his family—are the judges of the service. This open market creates a healthy feedback from the consumer to the professional educator. If nobody buys the Edsel, it will no longer be produced.

## THE POTENTIAL IMPACT OF ALTERNATIVE SCHOOLS

The concept of options in public education does not suggest that alternative schools would replace conventional schools; rather, alternative schools would complement the conventional. Educational reform is not at issue here. What is at issue is the degree to which communities can expand, through choice, the number and kinds of learning environments without increased funds, new buildings, or additional personnel. It is equally important to understand the educational implication and connotation of the term so frequently used in this book, the term "choice." What choice specifically *does not* mean is that teachers and students through daily whim "do their own thing." Freedom of choice in a democracy has never meant license, nor does it in alternative schools. What choice *does* mean is that teachers and students (usually parents and administrative personnel are also involved) in concert, participate in planning, designing, implementing, and evaluating the specific goals, activities, and content essential to the learning process. Through optional alternative public schools the ideals of our democratic, pluralistic society are now becoming essential ingredients of mainstream American education.

### Community

The differences within a single community among its people and their social, political, economic, and philosophical values are usually greater than the differences from one community to another. This makes community involvement in public education essential, since our schools can reconcile these basic differences within each community only when such involvement exists. All communities share common needs, and it is these common needs with which state and federal agencies are primarily concerned. But while education responds to common needs, its success or failure nationally can and should be attributed directly to the way in which each local community identifies, discusses, designs, and implements school programs consistent with its own uniqueness. Thus, communities will continue to be an essential element in school improvement.

Education is responsible for influencing the relationship between individuals and the community. A monolithic system cannot respond to the needs of a community and its pluralistic population; a plurality of modes of education can. In many communities where alternative schools exist, the community has significantly influenced the school program. The reverse is also true. School programs are beginning to influence community life outside the school.

Nearly 1,500 communities throughout the United States are currently planning, generating, or implementing optional alternative public schools. Community involvement has been essential in their origin, design, and operation. Open dialogue has resulted in genuine commitment to make schools more responsive to community needs. Parents, the most overlooked educational resource in every community, have frequently become active participants in the normal routine of alternative schools.

The ways in which communities become involved in the development of alternative public schools varies from community to community. A general community position on alternative schools is neither possible nor desirable because educational needs vary from one community to another. What is important is that communities develop alternatives to serve various clienteles, to meet needs not presently being met, and to expand the number of learning environments to accommodate a broader range of teaching and learning styles.

How an alternative school is started depends entirely on what segment of the community first senses the need and to what extent. Students were the first to press for alternative schools in Newton, Massachusetts, and Ann Arbor, Michigan. In St. Paul; Sharon, Massachusetts; and Tuskegee, Alabama, it was parents.

Teachers provided the impetus in Racine, Wisconsin, and Newport Beach, California, and administrators provided it in Seattle and Grand Rapids. With the aid of a USOE grant, the University of Massachusetts started alternative schools in Worcester and Pasadena. Community organizations started alternative schools in Washington, D.C., and Oakland. In Berkeley, Cincinnati, and New Orleans nonpublic alternative schools merged with the public school system. In Denver, Hartford, and Philadelphia several school districts cooperated in the development of alternatives. In Madison, Wisconsin, students, teachers, professors, and administrators planned an optional alternative public school. In short there is no single pattern. We believe the best approach is the one that involves the most segments of the community from the initial planning stage on.

If the community role in public education has been slighted, and in our judgment it has, the optional school concept provides new opportunities and challenges to renew community participation in education. Local involvement and commitment could result in more effective schools and more effective school-community relationships.


## Curriculum

Will we ever get away from the three R's (rote, regurgitation, and reward) in our schools? Not in alternative schools if we mean *basic skills*. Alternative public schools are not only emphasizing basic skills, including reading, writing, oral and nonverbal communication, and computation; they are also including technological, personal, social, and aesthetic areas, and human relations. Furthermore, these schools are systematically developing new and different curricula along with the equally important methods, human resources, materials, learning climates, and time utilization that often determine curricular effectiveness. Alternative schoolers are frequently confronted with the misinformed assumption that what goes on in alternative schools is something less substantive with regard to basic skills and overall curriculum than conventional schools. This is simply not the case. The "do your own thing" syndrome, which is often assumed to be the curriculum basis in alternative schools, has no more place in a humane, individualized, open environment than it does in conventional schools.

In observing all types of optional alternative public schools, we have found that they typically have comprehensive sets of objectives covering these six areas: 1) basic skill development, 2) cognitive development, 3) affective development, 4) talent development, 5) career development, 6) role development (citizen-voter, consumer-critic, parent-spouse).

In general, the curriculum in the optional school seems to be more comprehensive than the traditional curriculum of the conventional school, perhaps because tradition acts as a constraint on curricular change. The alternative schools, with little or no tradition, can be more responsive to the curricular needs of their students.

In its broadest sense curriculum includes these six components: persons, places, times, methods, materials, and content. Most alternative schools, in practice, consider *how* these components vary with the uniqueness of the people involved. Briefly, for example, "persons" refers to *all* people participating in the educational process (students, teachers, administrators, parents, and other community members). Teachers are becoming managers of learning activities, facilitators, and guides. Students, beyond being active participants in the learning process, are also involved in designing and implementing their educational activities. Students may become "teachers" of other students. Lay persons play a role, serving as resources, "teachers," and aides. Traditional roles are sometimes blurred, and an individual's role may change frequently. Above all, alternative schoolers perceive education to be a people business.

With regard to the "places" aspect of curriculum, clearly much of what is educationally relevant in contemporary times falls outside of the confines of school classrooms. Learning theorists state that most learning is acquired through experience. Furthermore, people tend to learn more readily what is relevant to their individual needs. Thus, alternative schools have expanded the variety and number of places available in which learning can take place. Of course, a formal classroom environment is suitable for some kinds of learning activities and for some learners.

The formal classroom ought to be viewed as *one* environment appropriate for some people at particular times. Hence, alternative schools do have some formal classroom activity. The basic difference, then, is that alternative schools are providing a variety of places in addition to the formal classroom as a means of curricular expansion.

Alternative schools provide opportunities for exploring, designing, and developing a broad array of learning facilities. These schools are using a variety of nonconventional facilities available within their communities. For example, the St. Paul Open School is housed in a remodeled warehouse. The Brown School in Louisville began in the lobby of the old Brown Hotel. Other schools have been developed in a separate wing of a conventional school, a few regular classrooms of an existing school, unused elementary school space, or in other available quarters throughout the community.

Utilizing "time" effectively in education is a concern that alternative school personnel are confronting. Learning activities are taking precedence over time. That is, learning tasks are determining time usage rather than having the clock determine the length of a given learning experience. This command of time is very essential since teaching styles and learning styles require variability in the amount of time needed for successful learning. There is no master schedule in some alternative schools. Individual schedules and time constraints are managed within an educational setting instead of starting with imposed constraints and subsequently maneuvering learning tasks to fit such constraints.

Variations in the "methods" dimension of curriculum are being explored in alternative schools. Teachers are encouraged to practice in a manner consistent with their talents, interests, skills, and training. They are encouraged to express their individuality in terms of teaching styles. The same is true with learning styles. Matching of the two is paramount if good teaching and learning are to take place. Teachers practicing any methodological technique are likely to be successful if that technique is a comfortable and natural one. But teachers also attempt to help students determine their learning styles—the ways by which they learn naturally and effectively. Doing what one does best in a climate conducive to the success of a learning activity should produce more effective teaching and learning.

When curricular opportunities are expanded by establishing alternative schools, the availability of "materials" is also expanded. Using community resources automatically offers a wealth of material for both teachers and students. Since students are involved in designing some of their learning experiences, they frequently bring materials or identify materials which will assist them in achieving successfully what they have set out to do. In schools-without-walls, city sidewalks literally become their hallways. Alternative schools necessarily capitalize on the expanded availability of materials, particularly as they relate to a changing and increasingly technological society.

And finally, with regard to "content," often thought of as the major component of curriculum, the significance of alternative school curriculum is based not upon the acquisition of new learning or new information, but rather the attachment of new meanings to information that is already known or readily available. In a technological society, it is impossible to teach or experience all of the new information available in any given decade. What is essential is acquiring skills which will enable people to deal effectively with the significance and meanings of new information. Being able to comprehend, adjust, and cope with new information is as important as the new information itself.

Educators have long recognized that the curriculum should be designed to meet local needs. In the 1950s and 1960s, the trend was to nationalize the curriculum. Alternative schools are bringing the communities back into the curriculum. More specifically, schools-without-walls, learning centers, open schools, and multicultural schools are creating closer community-school ties. Students in alternative schools are spending more time in their communities dealing with their own community's problems. Schools cannot continue to simply reflect the work-a-day-world, they must become the work-a-day-world—and become life itself.

Since one of the more philosophic questions in American education is the degree to which education should either lead or reflect the times and the society, alternative schools are beginning to question status quo education and mirroring society in favor of a leadership role in the improvement of American life.

# School Governance

One way to look at governance in education is simply to examine the various leaders in conventional schools. A school board makes basic policies, which in turn are administered by the superintendent and passed along to a principal who gives his subordinates specific directions. There are, of course, sporadic attempts to make the educational system somewhat democratic. Students councils are organized to raise money and sponsor student activities. Parents join the PTA, and in some schools teachers are committed to death, serving on powerless advisory groups. This is not altogether in vain. As a matter of fact, in many schools governance and decision making are processes which both teachers and students choose to avoid. It is easier to bitch when others make decisions which require only adherence but not the corresponding responsibility. Nevertheless, alternative school personnel report that some form of shared decision making is a basic concept of alternative, humanistic, and responsible educational programs.

Some people assume that alternative schools are leaderless, that no decisions are made, that no one is held accountable, and that what exists are various degrees of chaos. On the contrary, there is leadership, and important decisions are made which are both practical and essential to a democratically operated school. Who is involved in governance and decision making, how people become involved, and when and to what extent they are involved—these questions have as much uniqueness as the very schools they represent. The critical issue that those developing alternative schools need to realize is that all governance matters are determined through discussion in the planning stages so that lines of communications are clear, state regulations and laws are known, and that individual school policies are developed by those who will be subjected to their restraints or conditions.

All too frequently, processes of selecting, sorting, and promoting characterize present day public schools. Similarly, rules, regulations, and policies tend to be the central thrust of governance in most schools. One of the objectives of alternative schools is to create more humane environments. It goes without saying that when people are involved in the decision-making process, they feel less ruled. One administrator of an alternative school recently indicated that the critical thing about decision making, particularly from the students' point of view, is that students do not necessarily want the power implied in decision making, but they want the right to have the power involved in decision making. In other words, they do not want the responsibility for making all decisions; they want the right to participate in decision making on those issues that are most important to them.

Most individuals in alternative schools are interested in good and just decisions and governance. When there is honest disagreement, solutions are arrived at through an examination of the issue by those directly involved. At times negotiations and compromises are necessary just as in other aspects of society. Better decisions result when interested parties are involved in resolving conflicts.

## Student Evaluation

Alternative schools lack sophistication in the area of evaluation. (Many conventional schools do too.) To compensate for this situation, alternative school personnel have attempted to accomplish at least two objectives in evaluation. First, they are continuing to use conventional techniques and devices to gather and analyze data. Second, and more important, they are emphasizing the necessity of obtaining data from a variety of sources, not the least of which is simply to ask students and teachers for candid, personal responses about their educational involvement.

Since educational teaming is so much a part of alternative schools, team planning, team teaching, team decision making, and team evaluation are producing more comprehensive evaluation designs, if for no other reason (and there are some others) than they utilize a variety of talents, viewpoints, and judgments based upon what each person brings to a given task. For example, by expanding the choices for teachers and students and emphasizing that decisions about these choices should be shared, more information can be gathered before making the choices. Different people bring different sets of perceptions, resolutions, and solutions, all of which contribute to the evaluation process. The concept of choice must be educationally significant in determining the degree to which teaching and learning is, or is not, taking place.

Many alternative schools have abandoned grading but have increased the emphasis on the evaluation of students. Grading and rank in class have traditionally been required because colleges wanted both for admission. A recent study of colleges and universities revealed that the majority (over 650 four-year colleges and universities and over 700 two-year colleges) admit high school graduates without grades or class rank. Emphasis is being given to competence and performance, not to time spent in class. When an alternative school youngster's progress is compared first with himself and then with that of his peers, the information takes on new meaning. The trend in alternative schools is to evaluate student progress in that order. Perhaps the most important aspect of evaluation in alternative schools is the fact that the very nature of the alternative concept is so much more consistent with what evaluation is all about. Waiting lists to get in are longer, teacher feedback is positive, and community interest is rapidly on the increase. In Cambridge, Chicago, and Philadelphia the alternative schools send a higher proportion of their graduates on to college than do conventional schools in those same communities.

If the educational potential of alternative public schools does little more than to bring sharply to focus the need to diversify our schools, it will have served a worthwhile purpose. Public education will be better for what the concept of choice has given, not only in terms of teaching and learning, but in the ultimate goal of education—to help people live more effectively. No other educational concept or reform effort has had this dynamic potential. If the national trend continues, alternative public schools will exist in the majority of communities in this country before the end of this decade.

## PROBLEMS OF THE OPTIONAL SCHOOLS

While the development of optional alternative public schools may have potential for making school systems more responsive to their diverse clienteles, those who are planning, developing, and operating alternative schools today face a number of serious problems. Naturally, the extent and degree of these problems will vary from community to community, but here are some of the common problems that we have observed to date.

In some communities there is a stigma on the alternative school concept. Some people have a conception of the alternative school as a place to send somebody else's children. Because some vocational schools and career education centers have been dumping grounds in the past, because some alternative schools are attempting to meet the needs of dropouts and potential dropouts, and because in some communities disruptive students are being assigned (without choice) to an "alternative school," many parents are already convinced that alternative schools are not for their children. Other people may be more familiar with the nonpublic "free school," which was so much in vogue just a few years ago. They see the alternative school as a place where students and staff have unlimited freedom and where little is taught or learned. Whichever the cause, some administrators, teachers, parents, and community members may be suspicious of attempts to develop optional public schools.

A second problem arises when an alternative school is established prematurely, without adequate dialogue and understanding within the community and particularly on the part of the parents, students, and teachers who are to be involved. Sometimes an enthusiastic board member or superintendent attempts to start an alternative school without analyzing local needs. Or a vested interest group within a community may try to force administrators and board members to establish an alternative without adequately assessing community needs or planning sufficiently. Educational faddism may cause problems too. Just because another community has a successful alternative school is not an adequate reason for every other community to copy it.

Providing adequate planning time for the staff is usually a problem. While time for planning and program development is desirable when any new school is opened, it is essential if that new school is to be an alternative to the conventional. In some communities school boards sold on open education have authorized the construction of new open schools. But sometimes the staffs of these schools have not had time to develop a program before the schools open. Unfortunately, the result is usually a conventional program in an ill-suited building.

An unusual problem is overenthusiasm. In every community at least a few teachers, students, and parents want to get away from the conventional school. They know what they are fleeing from but not what they are fleeing to. In fact, they may have very different and conflicting ideas on what an alternative school should be.

The first alternative school in any community will be a novelty. Accordingly it will probably attract undue attention from the press and radio and television and, therefore, from the community at large. Many alternative schools even attract visitors from outside the community in large numbers. This overexposure creates problems. Some students, teachers, and administrators in the conventional schools are naturally resentful of the alternative because they feel that their schools are effective and are equally worthy of attention. Schools in their first year of operation, whether conventional or alternative, rarely run smoothly and usually have frequent problems. Too much media coverage too soon can make normal developmental problems appear to be major catastrophes to the community at large.

Any time directors of alternative schools gather, they mention the problem of evaluation. This problem seems to be closely related to the lack of adequate time for planning and development. When the school has a clear statement of purpose and when evaluation is integrated into the planning and developmental stages, the evaluation problems are minimal. But it is not unusual to find an alternative school already in operation with its staff just beginning to consider means for evaluation.

In many communities funding is a problem. Throughout this book we have emphasized that alternative schools must be designed to operate on the same per pupil budget as other schools at the same level in the community. If the alternative school is to be housed in a new building already planned and constructed for it, then it would follow the same funding pattern for opening any conventional school. But when this is not the case, and it usually is not, funding problems can be difficult. Considerable administrative planning and negotiating are usually required to transfer funds from conventional school budgets to the alternative school that will enroll students who would otherwise have been enrolled in several conventional schools.

In addition to these major problems—stigma, premature operation, inadequate time for planning and development, overenthusiasm, overexposure, evaluation, and funding—there may be a host of minor problems, including changes in marking and grading practices; student record-keeping procedures; transcripts and college admission procedures; teacher transfers; building codes; fire, safety, and health regulations; and transportation arrangements.

Some types of alternative schools have particular problems. The school-within-a-school faces an additional set of problems. It is difficult to have different rules and regulations for different groups of students within the same building. The problems that arise in this situation are well described by Robert Riordan in the fastback titled *Alternative Schools in Action*. The school-without-walls has a different set of problems. Some communities are not ready to have students scattered throughout the city during normal school hours. In one community city bus drivers refused to let students from the school-without-walls use school tokens in the middle of the day.

Many alternative schools have an additional problem: they are oversubscribed. More students want to attend than there is room for. The result is long waiting lists and some feelings of resentment on the part of those who were not admitted. Each alternative school needs to develop in advance fair and equitable admission procedures. Some schools use a lottery, others use geographic distribution, and some use a combination.

While there are no general solutions to any of these problems, they can usually be worked out by adequate preliminary dialogue among all segments of the community; accurate assessment of the need for alternative schools; sufficient time and resources for planning, development, and implementation; and sincere commitment on the part of administrators, teachers, parents, and students.

## SYNERGISTIC EFFECTS OF OPTIONAL PUBLIC SCHOOLS

The development of optional public schools has had a refreshing effect on professional cooperation among institutions and agencies related to public education. But the term *cooperation,* or even *service,* fails to capture the spirit of what is happening, for the relationships that have been developed do not fit well the usual terminology. We use the term *synergism* to describe this new kind of school-college-agency relationship because it conveys more precisely the idea that institutions and agencies working together can achieve an effect in public education they could not achieve alone.

In the past, state agencies and universities have attempted to provide services for public schools. Serving suggests a unilateral quality: one party giving while the other receives. As such, service implies that solutions to problems are handed down from state or university authorities. Also, service activities in the past have too often been useless exercises in which local schools have had no real initiative or commitment to change what they were doing, and the authority-consultant, who assumed no share of the risk inherent in his advice, has often not cared whether the school acted on his suggestions. This relationship also failed to offer opportunities for professional growth on the part of the university or agency personnel.

The synergistic relationships that have grown out of optional public schools are replacing the traditional service approach with a far more productive situation. State departments of education, universities, and professional organizations have joined with public schools to facilitate the development and improvement of alternative schools, and there has also been a positive inverse effect. In some places the development of alternative schools has contributed to significant changes in state graduation requirements, college entrance requirements, teacher education programs, and teacher certification. Nearly everyone has criticized teacher education programs and state and university graduation and entrance requirements, but as long as public school programs were generally uniform, there was little need for significant revision. Alternative schools have changed all that. State departments of education have had to respond to public schools that have developed new curricula that differed dramatically—not only from the conventional curriculum, but also from state requirements.

The Washington State Department of Education, recognizing a general dissatisfaction with graduation requirements and the significant changes occurring in both public education and society, developed a new set of *Guidelines for Developing High School Graduation Requirements.* These new requirements not only provided more flexible procedures for graduation, they also stated, "Alternative learning experiences should be provided for each student within each subject area." Other state departments have assisted school districts in developing alternative and equivalent ways of meeting their requirements. A state requirement of a year in laboratory science might be fulfilled by a course in experimental ecology or a student-initiated research project. The usual year-long requirements in social studies and English might be fulfilled by a series of minicourses or through independent study, or even some type of community internship at local television stations, courtrooms, newspaper offices, or other local agencies.

As state requirements have been relaxed or changed and as alternative schools have developed new curricula, new methods of evaluating pupil progress, new forms of evaluation, and other ways of monitoring learning experiences, colleges and universities have become more flexible in their entrance requirements and procedures. When David Johnston and Jackson Parker were starting Walden III, an alternative public school in Racine, Wisconsin, they discovered that the primary concern among parents was: Will my child get into college if he goes to this alternative school? They promptly sent off letters to all the state colleges and universities in Wisconsin and found that their students would have little trouble gaining admission. A similar situation was found in a survey by Don Glines when he was directing the Wilson School, an open alternative school in Mankato, Minnesota. More recently a national survey of colleges and universities found that the majority were willing to admit students without class rank, grade point averages, and the usual transcript of courses.

## Teacher Education Programs

Alternatives have also positively affected university teacher education programs. When public school educators met for the first invitational conference on alternative public schools at the Wingspread Conference Center in Racine, Wisconsin, in April, 1972, they discovered that of the multitude of problems facing the new alternative schools, one of the most critical concerns was teacher education. As school districts began to develop alternative learning experiences, it became obvious that there were few trained or experienced teachers available to operate the new schools. As one administrator put it, "In our entire school district, we found no one who had ever worked in an open school, much less a free school or a school without walls. Oh, we had a few teachers who had read John Holt and Herb Kohl, but nobody had the intellectual toughness and the down-to-earth-know-how to get the thing going."

Finding few teachers who possessed the skills to teach in nonconventional educational programs, some school districts tried to provide their own retraining programs; others simply let their teachers muddle through on their own. Lacking experience and skills, many teachers found the transition to alternative education so demanding that the burn-out rate was high. The educators at the conference cited the need for teacher training programs that related to the staffing needs of alternative public schools.

Responding to this growing demand for nonconventional teachers, a few colleges and universities have created teacher education programs that focus on emerging roles in alternative public schools. The task, however, has not been easy. Often it

33

has meant preparing completely new kinds of teachers with new skills for emerging roles that are poorly defined and still evolving. Trying to design a program to develop teachers for a variety of educational settings has likewise created problems. How could one program develop competent teachers for open schools, schools-without-walls, continuous progress schools, and others? In many alternatives, what we have come to call teacher has been transformed in dramatic ways. Entirely new roles have been demanded by the new schools. But while the task is far from simple, a number of teacher education programs are being developed.

1. *Indiana University:* Indiana University once had a monolithic program for the education of elementary and secondary teachers. Today IU students can choose from among over twenty alternative programs. They may choose to work in multicultural settings, urban or rural settings, or in programs preparing them to teach American Indians, Latinos, or other target groups. One of these alternative programs is a fifth-year program focusing on alternative public schools. The IU Alternative School Teacher Education Program was developed cooperatively by university faculty members and public school personnel. The students are all certified teachers who are interested in careers in alternative schools. The program is built around a year-long internship or residency in an alternative public school. Cooperating public schools provide the interns with a stipend and assume major responsibility for their field training. A public school teacher or administrator serves as an adjunct professor in charge of field experiences for the interns and residents at each site. Current field sites include Louisville, Kentucky; Seattle, Washington; Grand Rapids, Michigan; Racine, Wisconsin; and Oak Ridge, Tennessee. The students select a school setting that they feel is compatible with their skills and interests, and then work as teachers, as administrative aides, or in research and development projects. The IU students have been used by public schools to help conduct needs analyses of their communities, to help plan and develop new alternatives, and to help in strengthening and expanding existing programs. The program provides onsite training for interns, and the interns provide schools with a valuable talent resource for innovation and renewal. IU has also become a leader

in inservice programs for alternative school teachers and administrators; the IU workshops in alternative education attract educators from throughout the country each summer.

2. *New School for Behavioral Studies in Education, University of North Dakota:* The New School, while focusing only on elementary education, has become a center for teacher education programs in open education. The program has attracted large numbers of people who have completed liberal arts degrees and are seeking elementary teacher certification. A key feature of this program is its emphasis on retraining experienced teachers and renewing conventional schools. The program enables experienced teachers to return to the New School to learn open education skills while their classrooms are being taught by students in the graduate program. The schools become field training sites for teachers-in-training to test out their ideas while the regular teachers develop new skills at the New School.

3. *University of Massachusetts:* The National Alternative Schools Program has developed a unique relationship with a number of alternative public schools. The university provides comprehensive consultation, research and development, and staff training for cooperating alternative schools; the schools in return become training sites for prospective teachers. The program is currently working with alternative schools in California and Massachusetts. On the assumption that no one knows the best way to prepare each person for each teaching role, the program allows students maximum choice in "where, how, and for what" they will prepare.

4. *Mankato State College:* The Studies for Educational Alternatives is a program at Mankato State College in Mankato, Minnesota, which offers students an open alternative for teacher education. The program includes three individualized components: 1) The Experimental Studies Program for undergraduate general-education and nonmajor students; 2) The Experimental Master's Degree offering a completely individualized graduate program for both teacher and nonteacher candidates; and 3) The Wilson Alternative Lab School, housing programs from nursery age through high school. The Wilson School provides prospective alternative school teachers with valuable teaching experiences in a flexible, nonconventional educational setting.

35

5. *San Francisco State University:* Since 1970, the School of Education of San Francisco State University has had a program for preservice secondary teachers interested in alternatives. Field experiences are available in alternative schools and programs in San Francisco, Oakland, Berkeley, Mill Valley, and San Rafael. Seminars are held in which the field experience is explicated. On two occasions students have had opportunities to become involved, not only in working in an alternative, but in the organization and establishment of an alternative. The field experience is available either as paraprofessional or as student teacher or as both.

Teacher education programs also exist at the University of Pennsylvania, the University of Minnesota, the University of Cincinnati, Lehman College of CUNY, and an especially interesting program in humanistic open education at the University of Florida.

A number of other colleges and universities have initiated courses on optional public schools. Such courses can be found at Central Michigan University, California State University, Glassboro State College, the University of Colorado, Washington University, and the University of British Columbia.

Many alternative schools near colleges and universities with teacher education programs rely heavily upon those programs for paraprofessionals, interns, and student teachers. These schools have in turn had a very real influence upon teacher education programs.

## State Departments of Education

Besides the important work of revising graduation requirements and assisting schools in developing equivalent ways of fulfilling requirements, state departments have also conducted descriptive surveys of alternative public schools in half a dozen states and published state and regional directories. They have held or cosponsored regional and state conferences and workshops to help public school educators familiarize themselves with the idea of alternatives and to help them gain new skills and exchange information. The state superintendent's office in Illinois has gone even further. The state office has developed the Illinois Network for School Development, a program that when fully established will have developed new educational programs for no less than 135,000 students through forty-five affiliate schools. The network is primarily designed to act as a catalyst and a support system, and while it has provided ten school districts with $10,000 each for starting costs, it is working to maintain all alternative affiliates at existing per-pupil cost. The network enables each local alternative to develop its own priorities, but it emphasizes the need for career education, individualization, comprehensive evaluation, and equal educational opportunity for all. State departments in California, Florida, Indiana, New Jersey, New York, and Washington are also encouraging the exploration and development of optional public schools.

## Institutional and Organization Support

The development of alternative schools has also attracted the help of a number of diverse organizations and institutions. Professional associations such as the National Association of Secondary School Principals, the National Education Association, the National Elementary Principals Association, Phi Delta Kappa, the Association for Supervision and Curriculum Development, and the National Council for the Social Studies have all featured optional public schools in their journals. Alternative public schools have also been included on programs at annual meetings of the American Association of Colleges of Teacher Education, the American Association of School Administrators, the Association for Supervision and Curriculum Development, the National School Boards Association, and the National Association of Secondary School Principals.

Several new organizations have also been developed to assist optional public schools. The International Consortium for Options in Public Education (ICOPE) was created in order to help operating optional schools assist one another. ICOPE has done this through the newsletter, *Changing Schools*, position papers, a directory of alternative public schools, and through regional, national, and international conferences. Over 4,000 teachers, administrators, students, and parents have attended ICOPE regional and national conferences in the last two years.

The Center for New Schools, located in Chicago, has assisted alternative schools through the development of evaluation models and indepth case studies of alternative schools, and with a recent grant from the Carnegie Corporation, it is now assisting several schools districts in the Midwest to start alternatives.

The Experimental School Program of the National Institute of Education has funded alternative schools in Berkeley and Minneapolis and has developed evaluation models plus a body of research information on alternative schools.

Alternative schools have also attracted the support and co-operation of social agencies not usually associated with public education. In Bloomington, Indiana, the Community Action Program was instrumental in starting an alternative school in co-operation with the local public school district. In South Bend, Indiana, and Grand Rapids, Michigan, street academies were initially developed under the Model Cities Program and then incorporated into the local public school system. Other alternatives have been supported by local business and industry.

Throughout their short career, optional alternative schools have provided new avenues of cooperation between parents, students, teachers, and school administrators, and they have also caused communities, state agencies, organizations, and institutions to join together in a new spirit of synergistic cooperation and support.

## RENEWAL IN PUBLIC EDUCATION

During the last two decades monumental amounts of money, energy, talk, and print have been devoted to educational reform. Yet many feel that the schools of today are not significantly better than the schools of 1950. As Ruth Weinstock says in *The Greening of the High School:*

> This, then, is the condition which confronts us: though youth is no longer the same, and the world is no longer the same, high schools are essentially unchanged from what they were at the beginning of the century.

We assume that the term "educational reform" means a significant improvement that would affect a majority of the schools and a majority of the students. If this definition is correct, we must conclude that the much-heralded educational reform will not come in this decade, and in all probability not in this century. Educators and parents concerned about the need for more effective schools are not likely to discover or invent the panacea they seek.

Instead they will have to settle for the relatively random development of alternative modes of education which meet individual community needs. If the development of optional alternative schools continues to burgeon, this local response to local educational problems will have definite advantages over the panacean reform that many have been seeking. We like to think of this development as a strategy for self-renewal in public education.

Among the futurists there seems to be general agreement that the educational systems of the future will have to provide a wide range of learning options for all citizens. The wide-

39

spread but scattered development of individual alternative public schools will provide a foundation and a model for developing learning options that will be required by our future society. Meanwhile, establishing optional schools within the community is a simple and effective way to provide a total educational program responsive to the needs of all families in the community.

This strategy has the advantage of immediate impact. Any community where some citizens are concerned about the schools can plan and develop one or more optional schools now. Unlike major reform efforts, which require years of planning and development, the optional school strategy involves less planning and more action. Typically parents, teachers, and students in many communities start planning one year for a school that is in operation the following year.

Other advantages of this strategy have been pointed out elsewhere in this book. They include community involvement, low cost, low risk, accountability to the consumer, and increased commitment on the part of students, parents, and teachers to what is chosen rather than compulsory.

### The International Consortium For Options in Public Education

In 1971, after several meetings of educators involved in the development of optional alternative public schools, the International Consortium for Options in Public Education (ICOPE) was established. ICOPE is an ad hoc group of people and institutions which seeks to encourage the development of optional alternative public schools in public education in this decade. By 1974, the consortium had over 500 members from over forty states, five Canadian provinces, Australia, Denmark, England, France, Germany, Norway, and Sweden, representing several hundred individual alternative public schools, plus public school systems, teacher education institutions, state departments of education, individual students, teachers and administrators, community groups and individual community members, education related organizations, foundations, and other interested individuals and groups.

The consortium, with executive offices in Indiana University's School of Education, publishes a newsletter, *Changing Schools,* and acts as a clearing house for information on alternative public schools. The consortium sponsors regional conferences throughout the United States and Canada and plans program sessions for national educational conventions. The consortium also provides consultant services, intervisitation arrangements, personnel exchange, and other services to its members. Over 1,000 persons attended the consortium's First International Conference on Options in Public Education in Minneapolis in the fall of 1973.

Many members of the consortium were engaged in efforts to reform public education in the sixties. They now believe the development of optional alternative public schools provides the most promising strategy for educational renewal in this decade. While recognizing that the thousand-plus alternative public schools in operation today have not yet had significant effects on the mainstream of public education, advocates of alternatives believe that the development of options has significant educational and social potential.

## Conclusion

Mario Fantini said in a speech in Vancouver:

> The development of public schools of choice is the only major movement in American education today.

And Neil Postman wrote in *The Last Supplement to the Whole Earth Catalog:*

> All of the reforms that will take place in education in the next decade will have their origins in the alternative school movement.

Whether Fantini and Postman are right is not at issue here. For those of us who have worked with the development of optional alternative public schools in recent years, the potential of public education in the future is exciting. The development of optional public schools within a community:

1. Provides schools through choice rather than compulsion.
2. Provides ways to make schools more responsive to the pluralistic needs of the community.
3. Provides a structure for continued change and renewal.

4. Provides an arena for the trial of new patterns of organization, staffing, and financing.

5. Provides vehicles for the trial of promising concepts in learning and teaching.

6. Provides opportunities for new cooperative relationships among public school systems, teacher education institutions, professional organizations, and governmental agencies.

7. Provides strategies for the decentralization of decision making and control.

8. Provides an organizational structure that will be more responsive to change and to the needs of the future.

9. Provides a community forum for the reconsideration of all aspects of education.

10. Provides opportunities for students and teachers to have more significant roles in determining learning experiences.

Bruce Howell, superintendent of schools in Tulsa, Oklahoma, describes the prospects of alternatives clearly:

> As for me, I see unity through diversity. A diversity in educational design that will permit parents moving from Houston, New York, or Los Angeles to find a curriculum program and an organizational pattern amenable to their thinking. . . . Flexibility and diversity are difficult to manage but, to me, the alternative to diversity is educationally untenable. The alternative is standardization and conformity. It is untenable because now in education we speak of uniqueness, of individuality. This mandates alternatives.